Thoughts from the *Heart*

Frances G. Core

Copyright © Frances G Core 2020

All rights reserved. No part of this publication may be reproduced, stored in a retrieval system, or transmitted, in any form or by any means, electronic, mechanical, photocopying, recording or otherwise, without the prior written permission of the publishers.

The author has made every effort to ensure the accuracy of the information within this book was correct at time of publication.

For requests, information, and more contact
Frances G Core at FrancesCore@hispenpublishing.com.

Available in ebook and print.
Print ISBN: 978-1-944643-31-7

Cover designer: LaCricia A'ngelle HPP Designs

Scriptural References taken from Holy Bible King James Version unless otherwise noted

Thoughts from the *Heart*

Frances G. Core

www.hispenpublishing.com

This book is dedicated to all people. It is my prayer that you will be blessed by the messages the Holy Spirit has given me to share with you.

I give honor to the Holy Spirit and my sincere gratitude for the words He has given me.

Special Thanks to my daughter in law Lacricia Core and His Pen Publishing LLC for helping make this book possible.

Table of Contents

Let's Go Forward 1

Now Is Not The Time!... 3

Faith on Trial 5

Faith on Trial Part II... 9

Rejoicing in The Midst of Dire Circumstances 11

The "Word" Within You 14

The Benefits of a Gift: The Consequences of Sin 16

Give Thanks 19

The Present of His Presence 21

The Time of Refreshing.. 24

Celebrate Jesus, Celebrate Life 26

Chosen.. 29

Walk in Forgiveness 31

Let the True Church of God Come Forth....................... 34

What We Have Because of the Blood of Jesus 37

Getting to Know Him 41

Getting to Know Him Part II.. 43

A Holy Life: A Life Worth Living 45

To Know Him is To Love Him... 48

The Joy of Christmas.. 50

Are You Ready for The Coming of The Lord? 53
New Day New Life! 55
The Joy of Living in the Divine Will of God 59
Sharing God's Love 62
Christian Love 64
The Essence of Praise and Worship Part I..................... 66
The Essence of Praise and Worship Part II.................... 68
The Essence of Praise and Worship Part III................... 71
Great Is His Love 73
Keep Focused 75
The Danger of Legalism 77
All Praise Be Unto God 80
A New Beginning 82
The Final Call to the Church.. 84
About the Author 86

Let's Go Forward

Many days have come and gone with devastating tragedies, tests, trials, and sorrows of life. Yet we can be encouraged, and of a good cheer, knowing that our Lord and Savior Jesus Christ has overcome the world. Romans 8:37 says, "Nay, in all these things we are more than conquerors through Him that loved us."

Now we have crossed the threshold, into new beginnings. It's true, many suffered much injustice in the name of progress in our city, broken fellowship in the body of Christ (church); break down of the family structure; we have witnessed destruction of cities, homes, businesses by fire, earthquakes, and storms and the loss of jobs. Nevertheless, for those of us who remain, <u>"Life Goes ON,"</u> therefore let us forget those things that are behind and reach for those things that are before us.

Ask forgiveness of those we have wronged, forgive ourselves for the blunders and messes we made of our own lives; then above all, seek God's forgiveness. I John 1:9 says "If we confessed our sins, He is faithful and just to forgive us of our sins, and to cleanse us from all unrighteousness.

Praise God for another chance to amend our ways and our doings and return to the God of our salvation, whereby we may have the peace of God and peace

Frances G. Core

with God which passes all understanding shall keep our hearts and minds through Jesus Christ.

Now Is Not The Time!

People of God this is no time to panic or get despondent over what's going on in the world, attacks on the Body of Christ; and many other events that are going to take place.

It's time to do a self-examination and true repentance. Listen to what the Lord spoke through the prophet Hosea, although speaking to Israel, He is speaking now: "Hear the Word of the Lord, You children of Israel (America), for the Lord brings a charge against the inhabitants of the land: There is no truth or mercy or knowledge of God in the land. By swearing and lying, killing and stealing and committing adultery, they break all restraint, with bloodshed upon bloodshed. Therefore the land will mourn; and everyone who dwells there will waste away with the beast of the field and the birds of the air; even the fish of the sea will be taken away. Now let no man contend, or rebuke another; for your people are like those who contend with the priest (God's ordained authority). Therefore you shall stumble in the day; the prophet (false prophet) also shall stumble with you in the night; and I will destroy your mother (the nation)." Hosea 4:1-5

My people are destroyed for lack or knowledge, because you have rejected knowledge, I will reject you from being priest to Me (see First Peter 2:9) Because you have forgotten the law of your God, I also will forget your children. Hosea 4:1-6

But God also gave us a solution in 2 Chronicles 7:14 "If My people who are called by My name will humble themselves and pray and seek my face, and turn from their wicked ways, then I will hear from heaven, and will forgive their sin and heal their land." The Word of God to the people of God.

Faith on Trial
(Suffering of the Righteous)

Beloved, think it not strange, concerning the fiery trials which is to try you, as though some strange things happened to you.

But rejoice inasmuch as ye are partakers of Christ's sufferings, that when His glory shall be revealed, ye may be glad also with exceeding joy. (I Peter 4:12-13)

God has called every true believer to a divine destiny. To reach the divine destination He allows the believers to go through many obstacle courses, to prove or test their faith.

Therefore, the textual Scripture above, conveys the message to the believers that trials and sufferings are inevitable, if we (the believers) are to be transformed and conformed to the likeness of Jesus, in true holiness, through faith and obedience.

As we encounter the trials and sufferings of this life, we are not to fall as victims of circumstance, in sudden surprise as if something unusual occurred; since the Word of God teaches us in Psalms 34:19, "Many are the afflictions of the righteous: but the Lord delievereth him out of them all." Jesus said, "These things I have spoken unto you, that in Me ye might have peace. In the world ye shall have tribulation: but be of good cheer; I have overcome that world," (St. John 16:33). So, we are to know to expect being attacked by the world, Satan and yes even sometimes by other Christians, who have not totally submitted to the will of God. For this cause, the Apostle Peter exhorts us to rejoice as we share in Christ's sufferings, being faithful to Him: in doing so, the "Spirit of Glory: and of God is released in us and rests upon us, enabling us to persevere, "enduring hardness as good soldiers of Jesus Christ." (II Timothy 2:3).

So that there will be <u>no identity crisis</u> as to who we are or whose we are; suffering for righteousness identifies us with Christ according to Peter 4:1-2, "foreasmuch then as Christ hath suffered for us in the flesh, arm yourselves likewise with the same mind: for he that hath suffered in the flesh hath ceased from sin: That he no longer should live the rest of his time in the flesh to the lusts of men, but to the will of God."

That is, when one willingly suffers for the cause of Christ, the desire to sin becomes easier to resist and the desire to do the will of God the Father becomes greater. The same prayer Jesus prayed in the Garden of Gethsemane... "Not my will, but thine be done" (Luke 22:42), will be ours.

There are times when the sufferings seems more than one can bear, and prays for deliverance. It is not that God does not hear, because He does hear according to Psalms 34:15, 17. But there is a lesson to be learned and a greater glory awaits. Listen to what Hebrews 5:8-9 says of Jesus, "Though he were a Son, yet learned He obedience by the things which He suffered; And being made perfect, He became the Author of eternal salvation unto all them that obey Him." Christ learned by experience the suffering, cost and hardship that come as a result of faithful obedience. Yet, He became the perfect Savior and high priest after accomplishing His appointed suffering by death on the cross without sin, bringing salvation to all who receives and obeys Him. Only it does not stop there. Let us see what I Peter 5:10 says of the believers who endure suffering through faith and obedience, "But the God of all grace, who hath called us unto His eternal glory by Christ Jesus, after that we have suffered awhile, make you perfect, stablish, strengthen and settle you," <u>Now that is a blessing</u> my friends!

Suffering for righteousness will also increase the depth of the believer's joy in the Lord, (Matthew 5:10-12; Acts 5:41, 16:25; Romans 5:2-5), so much so that the believer looks beyond the problem or situation, but look unto Jesus the Author and Finisher of our faith, who for the joy that we may be perfect, and entire, wanting nothing, according to James 1:2-4

And be comforted in this, also: "A diamond cannot be polished without grinding, nor can a man/woman be perfected without hardships."

Frances G. Core

Scriptures to Ponder

Psalms 55:22
Proverbs 10:3
II Corinthians 4:17-18
Philippians 1:27-30
II Timothy 2:12
Hebrews 11:24-25
I Peter 2:19, 21
I Peter 3:13-18
I Peter 4:15-19

Faith on Trial
Part II
(Suffering of the Righteous)

To continue with the previous topic from the Scriptural Text: I Peter 4:12-13 "Beloved, think it not strange, concerning the fiery trials which is to try you, as though some strange things happened to you. But rejoice in as much as ye are partakers of Christ's suffering that when His glory shall be revealed, ye may be glad also with exceeding joy."

The more I mediate on these words of exhortation, I believe, not only will the enemy continuously hurl fiery darts our way, but God also brings us to the forefront or the frontline in spiritual battles as we "grow in grace and in the knowledge of our Lord and Savior, Jesus Christ." II Peter 3:18

When God directs our steps through wilderness experiences as with Jesus (Matthew 4:1-11; Mark 1:12-13; Luke 4:1-13), is where, I believe, <u>the rubber meets the road</u> in our faith walk, a place where the genuineness of faith is proven; a place where every true believer comes to know the security and protection of the loving Father as they persevere and remain faithful to Christ in the midst of the trial, whatever it may be or however it comes.

Frances G. Core

To remain faithful to Jesus Christ in obedience, brings glory, honor and praise both to the believer and to Him.

Scriptures to Ponder
Psalms 18: 2-3; Psalms 23; Psalms 27:5
Psalms 91; Psalms 107: 1-7, 20-22; Isaiah 40:28-31
Isaiah 41:10, 13; Isaiah 43:1-2
St John 15:4-5,7; Philippians 4:4-8
1 Corinthians 10:13; Colossians 1:23

Rejoicing in The Midst of Dire Circumstances

While thinking on the most unpleasant situations, that have befallen our neighbors, by the devasting destruction of Hurricanes, pandemics, unemployment; the heartbreaking task of having to move on after the death of a loved one, which has been felt everywhere, at one time or another, the words of the Apostle Paul in Philippians 4:4 comes to mind, it says. "Rejoice in the Lord always, and again I say rejoice."

Paul, as inspired by the Holy Spirit, wrote these words to exhort the church in Philippi, while he was in prison. Although he was in a bad situation, yet he was exhorting and encouraging others. This is my earnest intent toward all who read this book. The circumstances are different, nevertheless the meaning and the results will be the same: to God's glory; to our edification (up building or uplifting) in spirit; then for our glorification in Christ.

I am sure you can recall other dreadful events we have encountered as individuals and as a nation, in which our heavenly Father sustained us and gave us strength to go on, even when we felt within ourselves we could not.

There are two passages of Scripture the Holy Spirit guided me to, at a gruesome point in my life that I resort to, for strength and encouragement, in good times and bad: Isaiah 41:10 Fear thou not; for I am with thee; be not dismayed, for I am thy God: I will strengthen thee; yea I will help thee; yea, I will uphold thee with the right hand of my righteousness.

Isaiah 43:1-3... Fear not, for I have redeemed thee, I have called thee by thy name; thou art mine.

When thou passest through the waters, I will be with thee; and through the rivers; they shall not overflow thee; when thou walkest through the fire, thou shalt not be burned; neither shall the flame kindle upon thee. For I am the Lord thy God; the Holy One of Israel, thy Savior.

Not only do I receive strength and encouragement, but I have so much "peace" and as the song says, "floods of joy, oh my soul, like a sea billows roll" – that I cannot help but to "Rejoice in the Lord."

So you see, rejoicing in the Lord is the key- whatever the trial or test- to our coming forth as pure gold (Job 23:10). Outside of Christ or having weak faith- living in doubt and unbelief, one cannot truly rejoice. For only in Christ, does one have cause to rejoice as one reflects upon God's sufficient grace (2 Corinthians 12:9); His nearness (Hebrews 13:5); and His promises (2 Corinthians 1:20); above all else, His great love for us (St. John 3:16).

Even in the darkest of night; in the saddest hour, remember this: The joy of the Lord is your strength (Nehemiah 8:10); knowing that all things work together

Thoughts from the Heart

for good to them that love God, to them who are the called according to His purpose (Romans 8:28).

So, "Rejoice in the Lord always, and again I say R-E-J-O-I-C-E!"

I will bless the Lord at all times: His praise shall continually be in my mouth. "Psalms 34:1"

The "Word" Within You

"Let the word of Christ dwell in you richly in all wisdom; teaching and admonishing one another in psalms and hymns and spiritual songs, singing with grace in your hearts to the lord." Colossians 3:16 KJV

"Remember what Christ taught and let His words enrich your lives and make you wise; teach them to each other and sing them out in psalms and hymns and spiritual songs, singing to the Lord with thankful hearts." Colossians 3:16 Living Bible (Paraphrased)

In the crucial and devastating times in which we live, that will only get worse, as the end of age draws near, it is of vital importance to take hold of the word of God as never before, letting it dwell richly within.

The above verse of Scripture exhorts every <u>true</u> follower of Jesus Christ, to commit to memory the words Jesus said when under attack by the enemy (Satan), It is written, "Man shall not live by bread alone, but by every word that proceedeth out of the mouth of God." (Matthew 4:4) When having to make difficult decisions or choices, we can depend on the word of God and Christ by the Holy Spirit to guide us into all truth (St. John 16:13) making us wise and increasing us more and more in love for one another and in knowledge of Him.

Thoughts from the Heart

Having the "word" richly dwelling within, is allowing Christ, the Word and God, the Father (St. John 1:1), to live in you in <u>full measure</u> (St. John 14:23; 15:3,4). This is done through studying the word, continually (St. John 8:31; II Timothy 3:14), individually and group Bible study; meditating on the word (Joshua 1:8, Psalms 119:15, 23 & 48); praying for understanding and wisdom (Psalms 119:27, 34, 73, 125, 169; James 1:5,6), until you become so engulfed in the word as naturally as inhaling and exhaling.

When we pursue this experience, our thoughts, words, deeds, and motivation will be influenced and controlled by Christ; making us aware of the holiness of God by the Holy Ghost, creating a desire within us to be holy as God is holy (Leviticus 11:45; II Corinthians 7:1; I Peter 1:13-16. Then we can teach and encourage others in the word, in songs and hymns and spiritual songs, singing to the Lord with thankful hearts, as we live in obedience to the word.

Read: Psalms 119:11, 105; St. John 4:14; St John 8:31, 15:9; Colossians 1:9-11, 23; Colossians 2: 2, 3, 6, 7,8, 9 & 10.

The Benefits of a Gift: The Consequences of Sin

"For God so loved the world, that He gave His only begotten Son, that whosoever believeth in Him should not perish, but have everlasting life." John 3:16

As I think on the title of this devotion, Romans 6:23 comes to mind, it says, "For the wages of sin is death, but the gift of God is eternal life through Jesus Christ our Lord."

The "love", "favor", and "kindness" of God the Father bestowed upon fallen humanity, is the gift of his Son, Jesus (John 3:16). This act of grace is for everyone, but is only beneficial or profitable to us as we receive it and die to the flesh or sin nature (we all possess) by the Spirit (Word) of God in obedience.

Thinking in terms of a gift and wages, the definitions are very clear. A gift is something freely given and received. Wages are payment for work performed.

When you receive a gift from someone, you are not expecting it and there is no charge to you. It is given through the act of love for you, you did nothing to merit it. Note what Ephesians 2:8-9 says, "For by grace are ye saved through faith; and that not of yourselves; *it is the gift of God*: not of works, lest any man should boast."

Thoughts from the *Heart*

Now, on the other hand, wage is a recompense or payment for services rendered or loss (services not rendered) or the like. So then, it is natural to expect payment for services you rendered or pay for services rendered to you, neither is a gift. And surely you don't expect to get paid for something you did not do – loss wages.

Let's see what works are in the spiritual sense, according to Galatians 5:19-21, "Now the works of the flesh are manifest (made clear; to show plainly), which are these: adultery, fornication, uncleanness, lasciviousness, idolatry, witchcraft, hatred, variance, emulations, wrath, strife, seditions, heresies, envying, murders, drunkenness, reveling, and such like… they which do such things, *shall not inherit the kingdom of God*. When anyone takes pleasure in *the works of the flesh,* and continues in them, with no mind to repent and turn to Christ, the consequences of the penalty of death rests upon them, leaving them eternally separated from God.

If we are to receive the gift of God, i.e. eternal life, it is imperative for us to not let sin reign (rule) in our mortal body, to obey it in the lusts thereof. Romans 6:12. "…cast off the works of darkness (flesh) and put on the armor of light." Romans 13:12. II Timothy 2:19b says, "…and let everyone that nameth the name of Christ depart from iniquity." II Timothy 2:19. In doing so, we can enjoy the benefits of eternal life starting now according to Psalms 103:3,6,8,10,13,17,18. Deuteronomy 28:2-14; Psalm 91; Isaiah 26:3.

Frances G. Core

Never the less, the choice is ours.

Give Thanks

Bless the Lord, O my soul; and all that is within me, bless His holy name. Bless the Lord, O my soul, and forget not all of His benefits.
Psalms 103:1-2

As we approach each new day, we can look and see, even now, of how gracious the Lord had been toward us; better yet, how gracious He is to us at the present moment.

Despite the difficulties and tragedies that have touched our lives, especially recently, we are to say as David said in Psalms 68:19, "Blessed be the Lord, who daily loadeth us with benefits, even the Lord of our salvation. Selah."

Focusing on the opening Scriptural verses, the Psalmist, David, calls on his soul and every fiber of his being to give Thanksgiving and praise to God for all of His benefits and blessings. In the remaining verses is a list of God's blessings that show His love, mercy and kindness to all of His people.

David, like others in Scripture had faced many discomforting moments in his life, nevertheless, he did not fail to give thanks and praise to God, for His goodness and mercy; delivering him out of his sickness and diseases; giving him new life, joy, and above all- forgiveness of sin. Psalm 103:3-6

God has extended the same to us through His son, Jesus Christ.

We are to thank and praise Him, not only for what He does, but in all ways for who He is, Our everything.

O give thanks unto the Lord, for He is good; for His mercy endureth forever.

Let the redeemed of the Lord say so, whom He hath redeemed from the hand of the enemy. Psalms 107:1-2

Remember: "Everyday is a day of Thanksgiving.

The Present of His Presence

Behold, a virgin shall be with child, and shall bring forth a son, and they shall call his name Emmanuel, which being interpreted is God with us. Matthew 1:23

God's definition of a gift differs from ours. We tend to make the word "gift" mean things. Ask any child what he or she is getting for Christmas, they immediately begin to list things. Even grown-ups will say what things they would like to receive.

No one ever thinks in terms of giving or receiving "expressions of a loving relationship" from the other (husband to wife; parent to children; brother to sister; friend to friend, etc.) as a gift, which is what giving is all about. You give yourself to your loved ones in the gifts you offer. This relational giving is the heart of the matter, and that is how God defines the word gift; first, in terms of a relationship; second, in things. Here we have the divine definitions of gift giving.

When God gives a gift, that gift keeps on giving. When God gives, He gives Himself, and fellowship with Him is the purpose of His present.

We use the word <u>present</u> when we speak of gifts, but God speaks of gifts giving, he is speaking in terms of the word presence. So at Christmas, we celebrate "the present of his presence," in Jesus, within us. John 14:23, John 17:23; II Corinthians 6:16.

As we receive this precious gift by faith in our heart, we discover the life changing power of his presence, we begin to understand and appreciate the meaning of fellowship with him.

Coming as light into our darkness (St John 1:4-5,9), Jesus shows us the way home to the Father (St. John 14:6). We no longer need to walk as slaves to sin (Romans 6:1-8; St John 6:36), For we now have the lighted way to the city of eternal light, and because of the present of his presence, we are the children of light that shines forth in a darkened world (Proverbs 4:18; St Matthews 5:14-16; Philippians 2:15).

The fellowship we have with the Father in Jesus Christ provides freedom from sin, "and if any man does sin we have an advocate with the Father, Jesus the Righteous," says 1 John 2:1. Only through fellowship with God in Christ can we find the freedom that allows us to choose the way of life over the way of death. We are free to become all that God wants us to be by coming, just as we are (Isaiah 1:18-19; 1 John 1:7-9), to Jesus who justifies. Romans 3:24-26

Through this fellowship we also find favor with God our Father. 1 John 3:1 states "Behold, what manner of love the Father hath bestowed upon us, that we should be called the sons of God."

Thoughts from the Heart

Then we have faith through our fellowship with God in Christ. "Whosoever believeth that Jesus is Christ, is born of God; and every one that loveth him that begat loveth Him also that is begotten of him." 1 John 5:1. According to Romans 12:3, everyone has been given the measure of faith, it increases as we fellowship with God who gives faith.

Beloved, God has given us more than a thing called forgiveness. He has given us more than a thing called eternal life. He has given to us Himself in His son. He gives a relationship that results in forgiveness, eternal life, and all other things we delight to receive; all this is ours because He has given us the coming Christ to be with us.

Christ was and is the present of God's presence. He was and is the gift that goes on giving.

Thanks be unto God for his unspeakable "GIFT" II Corinthians 9:15

The Time of Refreshing

Repent ye therefore, and be converted, that your sins may be blotted out, when the times of refreshing shall come from the presence of the Lord; Acts 3:19

This is the Acceptable Year of the Lord, (Isaiah 61:2). He is sending forth, again, a great "OUTPOURING OF THE HOLY GHOST." (Joel 2:28-32; Acts 2:17-21), for such a time as this.

The church has lost momentum through: (1) Following after the traditions of men, making the commandments of God of none effect. (Matt 15:3-9); (2) Having a form of godliness and denying the power thereof (2 Tim. 3:5); (3) Tolerant of sin and unbiblical teachings (Matt. 24:11; 1 Tim 4:1, 3&4; 1 Pet 2:1-3, 12-14, 17-19; Rev. 2:14-15, 20); (4) Selfishness and unconcern for lost souls (Matt. 22:2-10, 23; 13-28; Luke 14:16-24; 15:4,8); (5) Division (denominations), when Christ is not divided (John 1:1; 1 Cor. 1:10-13; Eph. 4:4-6), Jesus prayed that we be one (John 17:20-23). We are one body in Christ, and every one members one of another, (Rom. 12:4,5; 1 Cor. 12:12-14, 20-27); (6) Having become more politically correct. (Gal. 5:3,4), than Christ minded (Phil. 2:1-5; 1 Pet 1:13-16).

Nevertheless, in spite of all our disobedience and short comings, God is saying to us, today, as He said to the

Thoughts from the Heart

children of Israel in Isaiah 43:18-19, "Remember not the former things, neither consider the things of old. Behold, I will do a new thing, now it shall spring forth; shall ye not know it? I will even make a way in the desert."

The "new thing," is a new time, a place of forgiveness, restoration, blessings and God's presence. Forgetting those things which are behind and reaching forth to those things which are before, I press toward the mark for the prize of the high calling of God in Christ Jesus. Philippians 3:13-14.

God is calling the church to WAKE UP according to Rom. 13:11-14; Eph. 5:14-16 and GET UP according to Isa. 60:1,2.

People of God, these things we must do, without reservations, if we are to receive the blessed promises of God and His true anointing, that will empower the Church of the living God and every true believer; enabling them to carry out the commission Jesus gave in Matt. 28:19-20; to witness, Acts 1:8, and to do the work of the ministry in Eph. 4:11-16, fulfilling God's plan and purpose on Earth.

Celebrate Jesus, Celebrate Life

The Lord is my light and my salvation, whom shall I fear: He is the strength of my life, of whom shall I be afraid. Psalms 27:1

"I am come that they might have life, and that they might have it more abundantly." St. John 10:10; When I think on the above verse, I'm reminded of the astounding production of "The Passion of Christ," produced by Mel Gibson.

In the previous lesson I wrote on the subject – **The Time of Refreshing**. I mentioned of God doing a "new thing" in the Earth. Well, I believe that He used this movie as a launching pad, for what He is doing in this, <u>final countdown</u>. Because of all the films produced on the Crucifixion of Christ, none have had such profound impact as this one. Many unsaved gave their lives to Christ. At the same time, many believers reevaluated their walk with the Lord, with an intense desire of a closer walk, as the Holy Spirit inspires them.

I did not see the movie, but I believe I can share in the same overwhelming experience. Sometime before the movie was shown on the screen, the Holy Spirit opened to me, through the Scriptures, the inhumane treatment of my Lord.

Thoughts from the *Heart*

As I was studying on the institution of the Lord's Supper, recorded in the Gospels, I continued to read all the events that took place, even after Jesus Christ's resurrection. But the crowning point was when I read the recording of the supper in 1 Corinthians 11:23-25, 29, and that's when it all came to light, especially the last part of verse 29. ... "not discerning the Lord's body." As I meditated on this, the Holy Spirit allowed me to view, through Him, the humiliation and mutilation Jesus endured, not for anything He had done, but for my sins and the sins of all mankind. It was so real, that I literally began to tremble as tears rolled down my face.

The Holy Spirit said to me, "When partaking of the Lord's Supper, remember, Jesus suffered in the flesh – the Just for the unjust. Keep in mind Isaiah 53; St John 3:16; Romans 5:6, 8-10, 17 and Romans 6:3-11. This Supper is not to be taken lightly or haphazardly, but with sincere devotion. Remember that it was God's redeeming grace, through the atoning blood of Jesus, that brought you to Him to give you life, and everyone who believes on His name. It is also a time of **rejoicing** and **thanksgiving**, knowing you have been redeemed, forgiven and delivered from the power of sin, escaping the wrath of God. "To take the Lord's Supper without self-examination, confessing and repenting of sin, makes you guilty of crucifying the Lord afresh." Hebrews 6:6

When the Holy Spirit spoke this into my spirit, my life in Christ took a whole new dimension, with an even greater desire and determination to be in His divine will: as I follow on to know the Lord in the power of His resurrection and the fellowship of His sufferings. Phil. 3:10.

It brought a deeper meaning of why I celebrate (Praise) Him. Space does not allow me to tell it all, but He has given me "**NEW LIFE**,"

Let me say it this way:
I will bless the Lord at all times: His praise shall continually be in my mouth. My soul shall make her boast in the Lord; the humble shall hear thereof and be glad. Psalm 34:1-2

I will extol thee, my God, O King; and I will bless Thy name for ever and ever. Every day will I bless thee; and I will praise Thy name for ever and ever. Psalms 145: 1,2

Chosen

As I was meditating on the goodness of God and all of His benefits to me, the Holy Ghost spoke into my spirit – CHOSEN – the title of this devotion. John 15:16

Looking at the word, chosen, the past participle of the verb choose, is synonymous to the word "elect." And it means it has already taken place.

None of us came to Christ because we decided to come, neither because we had gotten tired of the things (sins) we were doing and wanted to change.

It all started with Jesus Christ being the first chosen (elect) of God (Matt. 12:18; Isaiah 42:1,6; I Peter 2:4), He is the foundation of our election or of God's choice of us. St. John 1:12 says, "But as many as received Him (Jesus) to them gave He power to become the sons of God, even to them that believe on His name."

Ephesians 1:4-5 further clarifies our having been chosen, it states, "According as He hath chosen us in Him before the foundation of the world, that we should be holy and without blame before Him in love; Having predestinated us unto the adoption of children by Jesus Christ to himself, according to the good pleasure of His will."

God the Father had us in mind before the foundation

of the world, through the sacrificial death of Jesus, to bring us to Himself and make us a holy people, I Peter 2:5, 9&10.

Jesus said in John 14:6, "I am the way, the truth, and the life: no man cometh unto the Father, but by me. Then in John 6:44 Jesus says, "No man can come to me, except the Father which hath sent me draw him."

Beloved, we have been chosen by Jesus according to John 15:16; to be His "body." (Ephesians 4:12); His "church" (Matt. 16:18) and His "bride" (Rev. 21:9). We have been chosen individually, to come to Christ by faith, in true repentance, accepting God's gift of salvation in Christ (Ephesians 2:8, 3:17; Acts 20:21; Romans 1:16; 4:16; John 3:16) and brought together as "<u>one</u>" in Christ Jesus (John 17:21; Ephesians 4:4-6); making a conscious decision, daily, to remain in Him, submitting to His divine will in obedience.

The fulfillment of God's eternal purpose for the church is certain: Christ will "present it to Himself a glorious church ... Holy and without blemish." (Ephesians 5:27)

The fulfillment of God's eternal purpose for individuals is on the condition that, we continue in faith grounded and settled, and be not moved away from the hope of the gospel." (Colossians 1:22 & 23) Christ will present us "holy and without blame before Him" (Ephesians 1:4; Jude 24).
Thank God for being "CHOSEN!"

Walk in Forgiveness

"...And forgive us our debts, as we forgive our debtors.
Matthew 6:12

I was going through some keepsakes and I came across this "gem," a prayer written by a precious sister in Christ, who was much strength and encouragement to me in my walk with the Lord. She would always say, "you must wear this world as a loose garment." In other words, don't get so in tangled or so in love with the things of this world, that you can't easily slip out without being so deeply wounded, that you almost never heal. This even includes some relationships that can be devastating, both naturally and spiritually. She would also say, "You must be so careful or the devil will slip you a <u>mickey</u>" (a drug drink intended to make an unsuspecting victim unconscious.) I have experience that UNFORGIVENESS is one of his mickeys he slips in on believers easily, because he knows the fatal results it brings. Jesus said, "For if ye forgive men their trespasses, your heavenly father will also forgive you: But if ye forgive not men their trespasses, neither will your Father forgive your trespasses." What a gruesome condition we will be in, not having God's forgiveness and being eternally separated from His presence.

Forgiveness is the giving up of resentment or claim to requital on account of an offense. It is conditioned on repentance and the willingness to make restoration or atonement, bringing about the restoration of both parties to the former state of relationship.

PRAYER

Father, in the name of Jesus, I make a fresh commitment to You: to live in peace and harmony, not only with other sisters and brothers in the Body of Christ, but also with my friends, associates, neighbors and family.

I let go of all bitterness, resentment, envy, strife and unkindness in any form. I give no place to the devil, in Jesus name.

Now Father, I ask your forgiveness, by faith I receive it, having the assurance that I am cleansed from all unrighteousness, through Jesus Christ.

I ask You, to forgive and release all who have wronged and hurt me; I forgive and release them. Deal with them in Your mercy and loving kindness.

From this moment on, I purpose: to walk in love; to seek peace; to live in agreement and to conduct myself toward others in a manner that is pleasing to You.

I know that I have right standing with You and Your ears are attentive to my prayers.

It is written in Your word that the love of God has been

poured forth into my heart by the Holy Ghost, who is given to me.

I believe, that love flows forth into the lives of everyone I know; that I may be filled with and abound in the <u>fruits</u> of righteousness which bring glory and honor unto You, Lord, in Jesus name. Amen.

Scripture References

Mark 11:25; I Pet. 3:8, 11,12; Eph. 4:27,31,32; John 1:9; Phil. 1:4, 2:2; Rom 5:5; 12:10, 16-18; Col. 1:10

Let the True Church of God Come Forth

"Sanctify ye a fast, call a solemn assembly, gather the elders and all the inhabitants of the land into the house of the Lord your God and cry unto the Lord." Joel 1:14

"If my people, which are called by my name, shall humble themselves and pray, and seek my face, and turn from their wicked ways; then will I hear from heaven, and will forgive their sin, and will heal their land." II Chronicles 7:14

The world is in a great turmoil, Immorality, self-aggrandizement (a process of enriching oneself or making oneself powerful); destruction of cities, families and neighborhoods by violence; untrustworthy leaders in government, the workplaces and (yes, even in) the church are on the rise.

Despite the fact that these things are happening all around, God has given us the concrete solution, that lies within the realm of the "true church" according to the preceding Scriptures.

Look at II Chronicles 20:1-30, also. The children of Ammon and Moab came against Jehoshaphat and Judah and Jerusalem. Verse 3 says, "Jehoshaphat feared, and set himself to seek the Lord, and proclaimed a fast throughout all Judah. And Judah gathered themselves together, to ask help of the Lord: even out of all the cities of Judah they came to seek the Lord (verse 4). In verses 14 and 15 we read that: the Spirit of the Lord came upon Johaziel the son of Zechariah ... came the Spirit of the Lord in the midst of the congregation; and he said, "Hearken ye, all Judah, and ye inhabitants of Jerusalem, and thou King Jehoshaphat, Thus saith the Lord unto you. "Be not afraid nor dismayed by reason of this great multitude, for the battle is not yours, but God's." Take special note to verses 17 – 30, of how God gave Jehoshaphat and Judah the victory.

Although their battle was a physical one; our battle is both physical and spiritual. Is not the God Jehoshaphat and all Judah sought for help, the same God in whom we trust, worship and love: If so, let us likewise do as they did, for God is the same yesterday and today and forever. Heb. 13:8

Paul said in II Timothy 2:19, "Nevertheless the foundation of God standeth sure, having this seal, the Lord knoweth them that are His. And, let everyone that nameth the name of Christ, <u>depart from iniquity</u>." This is what we must do, depart from iniquity, seek God from the heart and not from the lips. It's not about our denomination (if it's established on the Word of God by faith in Jesus Christ), race, gender or status and certainly not about our political clout.

As the "true" Church of God arise and come forth,

armed for battle as in Ephesians 6:10-18; Knowing that, the weapons of our warfare are not carnal, but mighty through God to the pulling down of strong holds: Casting down imaginations, and every high thing that exalteth itself against the knowledge of God, and bringing into captivity every thought to the obedience of Christ: And having in a readiness to revenge all disobedience, when your obedience is fulfilled.

Then and only then, will we also have the victory through Jesus Christ our Lord.

What We Have Because of the Blood of Jesus

"Forasmuch as ye know that ye were not redeemed with corruptible things as silver and gold, ... But with the precious blood of Christ, as a lamb without blemish and without spot." – I Peter 1:18 & 19

Of all the things that I count dearest to me, my spirit becomes overwhelmed every time I read the above verse of scripture; and the ones following showing us what we have because of the "Blood of Jesus". Take note.

1. <u>The shed blood of Jesus made peace for sinners:</u> "He made peace through the blood of His Cross..." – Colossians 1:20. Jesus willingly took our place; He took upon Himself the form of man and in the flesh condemned sin in the flesh that we might have peace with God. Only those on this earth today, who are enjoying peace, have peace in their hearts through the shed blood of the Lamb of God. Apart from Him, there is no peace!
2. <u>The precious blood of Jesus Christ brings people into a new fellowship</u> "...Ye were without Christ, being aliens ... strangers... have no hope, and without God in the world: <u>but now</u>... ye who sometimes were far off are made NIGH BY THE

BLOOD OF CHRIST" – Ephesians 2:12,13. That shed blood of Jesus Christ breaks down man-made barriers and racial discrimination. Jesus told His disciples to go only to "the lost sheep of the house of Israel" but not to go into the way of the Gentiles – Matthew 10:5,6. <u>But Now</u> – the invitation is to "whosoever will". There is no difference, for the Lord is rich in mercy to all who call upon Him. And such mercy is made possible only by the shed blood of Christ.

3. <u>The blood of Christ cleanseth from all sin</u>: "If we walk in the light, as He is in the light, we have fellowship one with another, <u>and the blood of Jesus Christ His Son cleanseth us from all sin.</u>" – 1 John 1:7. The blood does not wash us from sin and leave it at that. The blood of Christ continues to clean us from all sin. Isn't it wonderful to know that our Savior does not push us out or damn us? He forgives our sin when we come to Him and confess that we have sinned: "If we confess our sins, He is faithful and just to forgive us our sins, and to cleanse us from all unrighteousness – I John 1:9.

4. <u>By the blood of Jesus, man is enabled to enter boldly into the presence of God, into the Holy of Holies</u>: "Having...boldness to enter into the holiest by the blood of Jesus...let us draw near with a true heart in full assurance of faith..." – Hebrews 10:19-22. Praise God, we do not need to go to an earthly priest and tell him our desires, neither confess our sins: but we can go directly

to the Lord, and through the shed blood of Jesus we contact the very throne of God in times of need and trouble, and find the help we need: "Let us therefore come boldly unto the throne of grace, that we may obtain mercy, and find grace to help in time of need" – Hebrews 4:16.

5. <u>The blood of Christ gives victory over the devil</u>: "…The accuser of our brethren is cast down, which accused them before our God day and night. And they overcame him BY THE BLOOD OF THE LAMB… - Revelation 12:10,11. Too often, we try to put up a battle against the devil, but we will never win if we fight in our own strength. However, if we fight the fight of faith depending upon Jesus and His shed blood, we cannot lose. The apostle Paul says, "Fight the <u>Good</u> fight of faith – I Timothy 6:12, therefore we win.

6. <u>The precious blood of Christ will never be forgotten throughout the endless ages of eternity</u>. It provides the theme of eternal songs: "And they sung a new song, saying, Thou art worthy to take the book, and to open the seals thereof: <u>for thou wast slain, and hast redeemed us to God by Thy blood</u> out of every kindred, and tongue, and people, and nation" – Revelation 5:9. Many religions of today have taken songs about the blood out of their songbooks. Men may refuse to sing about the blood; they may refuse to put their trust in the blood; they may laugh at the blood – but apart from the blood of Jesus Christ there is no salvation from sin:

Frances G. Core

> "And without the shedding of blood there is no remission" – Hebrews 9:22.

If you are reading this and you have not been washed in the blood, take the step of "faith", now –before the Lord, confessing that you are a sinner, ask Him to save you and He will! – Romans 10:8-11, 13. Thank God for the Blood of Jesus Christ Our Lord and High Priest forevermore. Other scriptures regarding what we have because of the Blood of Jesus Christ: - Matthew 26:28 and Romans 3:25. Remissions of Sins; St John 6:54. Eternal Life; Acts 20:28 Purchased by the Price of His Blood.

Getting to Know Him

Getting to know God is not because we want to of ourselves, but because God desires for us to know Him. Jeremiah 24:7 says, "And I will give them an heart to know me, that I am the Lord: and they shall be my people and I will be their God: for they shall return unto me with their whole heart.

Although God was speaking through Jeremiah the prophet of Israel's return from exile, after being carried away captive into Babylon; He is yet doing the same today, for us. We were all held captive in sin, by Satan and our own lusts. Upon our turning to God, through faith in Jesus Christ, He gives the desire to seek Him and promises us what we will find, according to Jeremiah 29:13-14a, "And ye shall seek Me, and find Me when you shall search for Me with all your heart. And I will be found of you saith the Lord."

Matthew 5:6 states, "Blessed are they which do hunger and thirst after righteousness; for they shall be filled (completely satisfied)."

Psalms 42:1-2 portrays one who yearns for God. As the hart panteth after the water brooks so panteth my soul after thee, O God. My soul thirsteth for God, for the living God: when shall I come and appear before God.

Frances G. Core

The following are some ways on how we may get to know God.

1. **Make Time For God.**
2. **Study The Bible Consistently.**
3. **Hide God's Word in Your Heart.**
4. **Fill Your Mind With Scripture.**
5. **Meditate on the Scripture**
6. **Dig Deeper Into Scripture**
7. **Pray**

The more you know of God and commit to His way, the more the transforming power of the Holy Spirit illuminates your life. Allowing your life to reflect the image of Jesus Christ, in everyday living.

Getting to Know Him Part II

Make Time For God.
Being that it seems we all live a hurry- up lifestyle, we must commit to make time for God. Get up a little earlier and start your day with Him, taking pleasure in doing so. Psalms 63:1 states, "O God, thou art my God; early will I seek thee: my soul thirsteth for thee, my flesh longeth for thee in a dry and thirsty land, where no water is." Commit at least 5 minutes a day, to begin with.

Study The Bible Consistently.
This is very important. Use devotional Bibles, and other devotion books containing scripture verses to get started. Read several verses or chapters, which requires a 10 to 15 minute commitment a day.

Hide God's Word in Your Heart.
Memorize the scriptures. Choose a verse to memorize, write it on a 3x5 inch card, put it in a place where you can often see it. Each time you pass it, review the verse, say the verse without looking at it, until it gets in your heart. Psalms 119:11

Fill Your Mind With Scripture.
Whether you are doing housework or driving around town, it is easy to let your mind wander. Listen to scripture songs, worship songs, or teaching tapes on

the Word; your spirit is lifted as you focus your mind on Jesus.

Meditate on the Scripture.
Joshua 1:8 tells us to meditate on God's Word day and night. To meditate on scripture - choose a verse or single concept, reflect on it and personalize it. I.e. make it your own; putting your name and situations into it. Consider each word and its meaning. Then ponder over their implications and how you should respond.

Dig Deeper Into Scripture.
Like one who searches for valuable treasure, never gives up until it is found, especially, when he is told the treasure is in a certain location. He searches diligently until he succeeds, sparing no pain nor time. So should it be when searching out the "richer treasures: of the Word of God. Laying hold on every promise God has made. Many treasures are available for discovery and personal application, but can only be found when we search diligently for them.

Pray.
Proverbs 3:6 In all thy ways acknowledge Him, and He shall direct thy paths. Mark 11:24 Jesus says, "Therefore I say unto you, whatsoever things ye desire, when ye pray, believe that ye receive them, and ye shall have them."

A Holy Life:
A Life Worth Living

As we have been brought into another day and have been given another chance for a fresh start in this life, by the divine grace and tender mercies of God the Father through Jesus Christ, his Son and the Holy Spirit, his wonder-working power, to whom I give praise, glory, honor with thanksgiving: I want to bring your attention to I Peter 1:13-17 from the Amplified Bible, "So brace up your minds; be sober (circumspect, morally alert): set your hope wholly and unchangeably on the grace (divine favor) that is coming to you when Jesus Christ (Messiah) is revealed. Live as children of obedience to God; do not conform yourselves to the evil desires that governed you in your former ignorance [when you did not know the requirements of the Gospel]. 15. But as the One who called is holy, you yourselves also be holy in all your conduct and manner of living. 16. For it is written, you shall be holy, for I am holy. 17. And if you call upon Him as [your] Father who judges each one impartially according to what he does [then you should conduct yourselves with true reverence throughout the time of your temporary residence (stay) [on the earth, whether long or short].

Dear friends this call to holy living or holiness is more than just being saved; more than an affiliation with any religious sect. It is an ongoing experience in our relationship and fellowshipping with our heavenly Father, who hath called us with a holy calling (II Timothy 1:9), to fulfill. His purpose in the earth, made known to us through Jesus Christ. It is the transforming of our lives as we willingly commit and submit ourselves to the Will of God, by the power of the Holy Ghost. Who lives in us.

Through this transforming power of the Holy Ghost... "everyone who names the name of Jesus, depart from iniquity (II Timothy 2:19); Setting our affections on things above, not on things on the earth. Because we are dead, and our lives are hidden with Christ in God. (Colossians 3:2,3); And we through the Spirit, mortify the deeds of the body, (Romans 8:13); presenting our bodies a living sacrifice, holy, acceptable to God. ...Not conforming to the world, but being transformed by the renewing of our minds, proving what is that good, and acceptable (pleasing) and perfect will of God. (Romans 12:1,2).

If living holy in the earth in this life was impossible, then Jesus who is our perfect example, came and gave His life in vain, (which He did not for me and countless others) and God the Father lied (which is impossible according the Numbers 23:19 to us in II Corinthians 6:16-18)

I am truly convinced in my heart, that holy living is possible not by our doings or on our merits, but by the true and living God who is faithful to everything He has said, when we obey Him.

Isaiah 1:19-20 says, "If ye be willing and obedient, ye

shall eat the good of the land; But if ye refuse and rebel, ye shall be devoured with the sword: for the mouth of the Lord hath spoken it."

Jesus said in St. Luke 6:46 "And why call ye me, Lord, Lord, and do not the things which I say?"

Therefore, what makes <u>A Holy Life: A Life Worth Living</u>. Comes through our obedience to God, the Holy One.

I appeal to everyone who has not submitted wholly unto the Lord God, <u>Do It Now</u>, do not live beneath your privilege any longer, you can be holy.

To those who has submitted, I admonish you to remain in this grace of God, no matter what comes or what goes. Don't give in nor give up. Don't compromise the gospel because of hardships, persecution, being cast out of certain organizations or affiliations because of righteousness.

It will be worth it all when we see Jesus.

To Know Him is To Love Him

I previously wrote on the topic – Getting to Know Him. The words God spoke in the scriptural text of that writing (Jeremiah 24:7) had a massive impact in my spirit. I began to reflect on my own life, how the spirit moved upon my heart, convicting me of my sins. I realized how helpless and hopeless I was without Christ in my life. Oh, I was attending church, held many positions, I was very dutiful (religious), gave tithes and offering, but my heart was not right with God. I would hear the Word, read the Word, but did not "OBEY" the Word. Then one day, God; through the Holy Spirit opened my heart to Him; not only did I realize what a sad condition I was in- separated from God- going to church, but did not have the "TRUE" church of Jesus within.

God allowed me to get a glimpse of the Cross- Jesus hanging there for my sins (yes, I know he died for everyone, but at this point it was personal). Isaiah 53; St. John 3:16; Romans 5:1-11 and many other passages of scripture really opened God's love to me. Every time I think on Romans 5:5-6, 8-10 my spirit becomes overwhelmed, it says, "And hope maketh not ashamed; because the love of God is shed abroad in our hearts by the Holy Ghost which is given unto us. For when we were yet without strength, in due time Christ died for the ungodly. V.8 God commendeth His love toward us,

Thoughts from the *Heart*

in that, while we were yet sinners, Christ died for us. V.10 For if, when we were enemies, we were reconciled to God by the death of his Son, much more, being reconciled, we shall be saved by His life."

As the Father draws us to Himself (St. John 16:8-11; II Corinthians 5:18-19) our hearts are made receptive to God's love, through the redeeming grace in Jesus Christ at Calvary. And as we draw near to God with a true heart, in full assurance of Faith (Hebrews 10:22), experiencing His love and mercy, growing in grace and in the knowledge of Jesus Christ, the more we love Him.

We come to know and love Him through his chastisement, when we err or disobey His commandments for Hebrews 12:6 tells us, "For whom the Lord loveth he chastiseth, and scourgeth every son whom He receiveth.

The more we come to know and love Him through studying His Word, applying it to our everyday life, regardless of the test and trials that come our way, He assures us of His love for us. Our love grows deeper and stronger for Him.

The Joy of Christmas

One of the "joys" of Christmas is "Toy Assembly 101." Late Christmas Eve, you take "it" out of the box -- Whatever "it" is -- read the so-called simple instructions ALWAYS including the magic words, "NO assembly required" OR "Easy assembly instructions enclosed" -- and the fun begins! You can't find all the parts, the parts don't fit together, you read and reread the directions, you count and recount the parts, you hit your left thumb with the hammer held by your right thumb -- you let out a scream -- and the nightmare begins! Remember?

More than 2000 years ago, a carpenter's life was turned upside down by the news that his betrothed was with child -- not his! The child was the Son of God, promised by the prophets of old, and Joseph was about to become the early caregiver of the Lord Jesus Christ. And a loving care giver, this carpenter was -- can you see him making wooden toys for Little Boy Jesus? Can you see him patiently showing Young Teen Jesus the "tricks of the trade," so He too, could become a GOOD carpenter from Nazareth?

Jesus, the CARPENTER? - Joseph, you better forget the dreams you hold in your heart for this young charge -- God has bigger dreams for Him! But wait... those plans STILL include being a Carpenter -- His shop has just been relocated to heaven's halls! He's the heavenly Carpenter who puts things together, who fixes what's wrong, who makes it brand new...who can take the broken things of your life, reassemble and restore all the pieces, and bring love and joy back to your life.

AND like all good carpenters, He knows how to "hit the nail on the head"...whatever you need, whatever repair is in order, you can open His Word and find the precise word you need to hear from His holy lips. The answer may be in a song or verse or a "word in season" from a friend that finds its way into your heart - and you KNOW the Carpenter has been at work! His shop never closes -- there's no charge for His services -- and He does incredible work!

Now believe it! Let the Christmas carpenter, skillful Workman in your life, have full control. Give Him all the broken pieces- He wants to fix whatever's wrong, to assemble all the parts, put them back in working order, and place You on display before the world as a heavenly-crafted person, repaired and renewed by heaven's Workman, the Christmas carpenter from Nazareth who is YOUR Savior and Lord.

Scripture: "For we are his workmanship, created in Christ Jesus unto good works, which God hath before ordained that we should walk in them (Ephesians 2:10)."

Prayer: "Lord, thanks for working on me! You never discard or throw me away as junk; you restore, renew, and reveal to me Your everlasting skill in "making it over" with Your skillful hands...I place myself in YOUR carpenter shop-- fix what's wrong, make ME anew, and may I display the beauty of your work, in Jesus' Name, Amen."

Are You Ready for The Coming of The Lord?

As I was reading Matthew 24 (the entire chapter) I began to visualize the things that are happening in our nation and around the world.

Jesus said in verse 8, "All these are the beginning of sorrow." Then in verse 12, He says, "And because lawless will abound, the love of many will grow cold."

This is taking place now people, all around us 24/7 but God has given us a solution, a way out in 2 Chronicles 7:14 "If My people who are called by My name will humble themselves, and pray and seek My face, and turn from their wicked ways, then I will hear from heaven, and will forgive their sin, and heal their land."

I think on these Scriptures often, as I pray for men everywhere, because I know in my heart that any day now, Jesus will be returning to this earth, I want to be ready to be caught up to meet Him, when He comes, what about you?

Colossians 3:1-4 admonished us, "If then you were raised with Christ, seek those things which are above, where Christ is, sitting at the right hand of God. Set your mind on things above, not on things on the earth. For you died, and your life is hidden with Christ in God.

When Christ Who is our life appears, then you also will appear with Him in glory."

If you have already received Jesus, "so walk in Him, rooted and built up in Him and established in the faith, as you have been taught, abounding in it with thanksgiving." (Colossians 2:6-7).

Sinner's Prayer

But to you who have not confessed Jesus Christ, you can this very moment, pray: **Dear God, I know that I am a sinner, I confess with my mouth Jesus as Lord, and believe in my heart that You, raised Jesus from the dead, Lord, come into my life, live in me, make me what You want me to be, thank You, Father, for forgiving me for all my sin, in Jesus' name.**

New Day New Life!

Oh, give thanks unto the Lord, for He is Good! For His mercy endures forever.

The Lord has kept us and brought us again through many trials, difficulties, disappointments and disasters. Yet, our heavenly Father has caused us to triumph. I can truly say as the song writer said in this song, "For every mountain, you brought me over; for every trial, you brought me through; for every blessing, hallelujah, for this I give you praise." The more I think on God's goodness, loving-kindness, mercy, His faithfulness and His awesomeness. I know there's none like Him. He is the true living God, the only wise God our Savior. All praise and glory belongs to Him, for He alone is worthy.

Oh, how amazingly sweet and good God is, that He is mindful of us (Ps. 115:12). It is for this cause, as we begin afresh, as children of God, affirm our commitment to Him. If, perhaps, any of us as Christians, have forgotten our covenant promise, became slack and half-hearted in our devotion to Christ, let us freely admit that we have sinned and confess our sins. He is faithful and just (true to His nature and promises) and will forgive our sins [dismiss our lawlessness] and [continuously] cleanse us from all unrighteousness [everything not in conformity to His will in purpose, thought and actions]. (1 John 1:9, AMP Bible).

Frances G. Core

After confessing and receiving forgiveness by faith, let us forget what lies behind, straining forward to what lies ahead...pressing on toward the goal to win the [supreme and heavenly] prize to which God in Christ Jesus is calling us upward (Phil. 3:13-14, AMP Bible). Hebrews 12:1-2 says, "Let us strip off and throw aside every encumbrance (unnecessary weight) and that sin which so readily (deftly and cleverly) clings to and entangles us, and let us run with patient endurance and steady and active persistence the appointed course of the race that is set before us. Looking away [from all that will distract] to Jesus, who is the Leader and the Source of our faith [giving the first incentive for our belief] and is also its Finisher [bringing it to maturity and perfection]"

Yes, Jesus endured all the greater opposition and bitter hostility, so that we won't lose heart and faint in our minds (Heb. 12:3). Give Him praise and glory!

To you, who have not received Jesus Christ as Savior and Lord of your lives, the time is now. No matter who you are, what you have done or your status in life, you too, can be partakers of this "Great Grace."

Let's see what Isaiah 1:18-19 says, "Come now, and let us reason together," says the Lord, "Thought your sins are like scarlet, they shall be as white a snow; Though they are red ike crimson, they shall be as wool. If you are willing and obedient, You shall eat the good of the land." (NKJV Bible)

Thoughts from the Heart

Don't refuse Him (Jesus) as this passage of scripture continues, verses 20-21 warns: "But if you refuse and rebel, you shall be devoured with the sword; for the mouth of the Lord has spoken."

Receive Jesus today, Today is the day that salvation has come to you.

Make haste! "Seek ye the Lord while He may be found, call upon Him while He is near. Let the wicked forsake his way and the unrighteous man his thoughts; Let him return to the Lord; and He will have mercy on him; and to our God, for He will abundantly pardon" (Isaiah 55:6-7).

If you are reading this devotion and have been touched in your heart, I invite you to pray this prayer:

Father, in the name of Jesus, I come to you, now. I realize that I am a sinner and I cannot save myself. And because it is not your will for me to be lost, you sent your Son, Jesus to die for me. Now, on the truth of your word, Rom. 10:9-13; I confess with my mouth and believe in my heart that you raised Jesus from the dead...and whosoever shall call on the name of the Lord, shall be saved. I call on you, now, Father forgive me for all my sins. I open my heart to you, come into my life. Cleanse me with your Spirit, that I may live holy and pleasingly to you. Thank you, Jesus for giving your life for me. I receive you by faith as my Savior and I make you Lord of my life. Amen.

Frances G. Core

Now ask God to lead you by the Holy spirit, to a Bible believing church, where His word is taught in the fullness; feeding you with knowledge and understanding (Jer. 3:15); that you may grow in grace and in the knowledge of Jesus Christ (II Pet. 3:18).

May God bless and prosper you in every area of your life.

The Joy of Living in the Divine Will of God

Great is the Lord, and greatly to be praised… Psalms 48:1

I praise God for His bountiful blessings and His immeasurable, immutable grace; He has given to us, through His son, Jesus Christ, our Lord. He has brought us, once again into another day by His own divine power, of His own will, "Oh, bless His name."

Many have made "Resolutions" that will most likely be forgotten within weeks. Then there are some, who will strive to live up to the resolutions they made, on their own strength, not considering the will of God in their lives, only to fall into deep despair and become even more dishearten.

I want to appeal to some and impress upon others, the unquenchable "Joy of Living In The Divine Will of God" It is not some kind of hocus-pocus neither is it a fly-by-night encounter, but a real true to life experience, that will last throughout eternity.

Jesus said, "Abide in me, and I in you. As the branch cannot bear fruit of itself, except it abide in the vine; no more can ye, except ye abide in me.

I am the vine, ye are the branches; He that abideth in

me and I in him, the same bringeth forth much fruit: for without me ye can do nothing.

If ye abide in me and my words abide in you, ye shall ask what ye will, and it shall be done unto you.

If ye keep my commandments, ye shall abide in my love; even as I have kept my Father's commandments, and abide in His love.

These things have I spoken unto you, that my joy might remain in you, and that your joy might be full. St. John 15:4-5, 7,10-11

In the beginning of this teaching, Jesus speaks of Himself as "the vine"; His Father as "the husbandman"; the believers as "the branches." He is laying the foundational principle that governs the saving relationship of Himself and the believers. When we, as believers, continue in this relationship by: drawing near to God, with a true heart, in full assurance of faith, having our hearts sprinkled from an evil conscience and our bodies washed with pure water (Hebrews 10:22); seeking the Kingdom of God and His righteousness (Matthew 6:33); submitting ourselves to God (James 4:7); and humbling ourselves under the mighty hand of God (I Peter 5:6); loving and obeying His commandments (St. John 14:15; 15:9-10), the more Jesus will manifest Himself to us, live in us and impart within us His divine power, fulfilling His joy in our hearts, causing our joy to be full and complete.

Friends, apart from abiding in Jesus Christ and His words

Thoughts from the Heart

in us, we will never experience the fullness of joy in His presence and the pleasures at His right hand. (Psalms 16:11)

So, instead of making resolutions every year or turning over a new leaf, some may say, which in reality it is the same old leaf, make this resolution once and for all: I will abide in Jesus, and let His words abide in me so that I may know the "joys of living in the divine will of God.

Have a blessed and prosperous day.

Sharing God's Love

One of the most learned and quoted verse of Scripture, taught from childhood, besides Genesis 1:1 and St. John 11:35, is St. John 3:16, "for God so loved the world, that he gave his only begotten Son, that whosoever believeth in Him should not perish, but have everlasting life". This profound verse of Scripture opens to us the very heart of God to all mankind, the "gracious gift" of His son, Jesus. It is by faith in His virgin birth and His sacrificial death at Calvary, that we can be restored to that "holy" state we had with the Father, before Adam sinned, bringing sin, sickness, and death to everyone, even the destruction and perversion we see in the world.

Yes, we were in the clutches of the enemy (Satan), not only facing physical death, but the everlasting sentence of death and hell, banished from the presence of God, without "hope", forever.

Then came "love" according to Romans 5:8-10: "But God commendeth His love toward us, in that, while we were yet sinners, Christ died for us. Much more then, being now justified by His blood, we shall be saved from wrath through Him. For it, when we were enemies, we were reconciled to God by the death of His Son, much more, being reconciled, we shall be saved by His life."

We, who are ambassadors for Christ, have received His love and continuously receive His love, are to share His

Thoughts from the Heart

love with those who are yet in darkness, bound with the chains of sin and death.

Let us not be as the scribes and Pharisees in Matthew 23:1-23, of whom Jesus called them by a few choice names, pronouncing "woe" on them. They were religious: "Having a form of godliness, but denying the power there of". (II Timothy 3:5), the verse goes on to say, "from such turn away".

But let us, "speak the truth in love", says Ephesians 4:15, always keeping in mind that, we, in time past: "were sometimes darkness..." Ephesians 5:8 and walked according to the course of this world, according to the prince of the power of the air; the spirit that now worketh in the children of disobedience: among whom also we all had our conversation (way of life) in times past in the lusts of our flesh, fulfilling the desires of the flesh and of the mind: and were by nature the children of wrath even as others. But God, who is rich in mercy, for His great love wherewith He loved us. Even when we were dead in sins, hath quickened us together with Christ, "by grace we are saved," Ephesians 2:2-5.

With this in mind and seeing the time and conditions of which we live, knowing that the "End" is nigh causes a yearning in my heart to those outside of the ark of safety (out of Christ).

So I admonish every "true believer" to stand strong, in the power of His might. Share His love, with joy and great enthusiasm.

Christian Love

"And I have declared to them Your name and will declare it, that the love with which you loved me may be in them and I in them". John 17:26

A Christian is a follower of Jesus Christ; a believer, a saint, a brother.

Love is the high esteem God has for His children and the high regard the children of God return to Him and to other people.

There are two distinct words for love noted in Scripture: (1) Phileo meaning "to have ardent (eager, fervent, passionate or burning) affection and feeling an impulsive (tendency to act on impulse, pushy, sudden urgency to act) type of love. (2) Agape – meaning to have esteem or high regard. It is this love – the Agape – God's love, the very nature of God- "God is love" (I John 4:8, 16) in which the Christian love is deeply rooted. A love that surpasses our power of understanding (Eph. 3:19); a love that is everlasting (Jer. 31:3) and free (Hos. 4:4); it is a sacrificial love (John 3:16) that endures to the end. (John 13:1).

It is the Agape (love) of God that has been poured out in our hearts by the Holy Ghost who has given to us. (Rom. 5:5), enabling us to let brotherly love continue (Rom. 12:10; Heb. 13:1; II Pet. 1:7). A love that goes

Thoughts from the Heart

beyond natural blood brothers to the brotherhood of true believers – "the God" (Eph. 2:19; I Pet. 2:17; 3:8).

As Christians, we are a brotherhood in the service of Jesus Christ (Matt. 23:8); a family made up of those who do the will of God (Matt. 12:50; Mark 3:35; Luke 8:21).

Jesus said, "A new commandment I give to you, that you love one another; as I have loved you, that you also love one another. By this all will know that you are my disciples, if you have love one for another". (John 13:34-35).

Christian love goes beyond brotherhood, to all people. Matt 5:47 says, "If you greet your brethren only what do you do more than others? Do not even the tax collectors do so?

Christian love prompts the believer to love your enemies, bless those who curse you, do good to those that hate you and pray for those who spitefully use you and persecute you. (Matt. 5:44)

True love is like oil to the wheel of obedience, enabling us to run the way of God's commandments (Ps. 119:32; John 14:21,23).

Much Love in Jesus' Name

The Essence of Praise and Worship Part I

"As the deer pants for the water brooks, so pants my soul for You, O God. My soul thirsts for God, for the living God. When shall I come and appear before God? Psalm 42:1-2

There is a sense of urgency for the body of Christ to recapture the vital importance and true meaning of "praise and worship".

The Bible has prescribed specific forms that are an important part of the believer's devotion to God. Far too long these certain elements of worship have been neglected – "spirit and truth."

Jesus said, "...the hour is coming, and now is when the true worshippers will worship the Father in spirit and truth; for the Father is seeking such to worship Him. God is a spirit and those who worship Him <u>must</u> worship in spirit and truth. John 4:23-24.

It is for the true believers to always remember what God, through Jesus Christ, has done for them, by Jesus giving His life that they might have life and life more abundantly. (John 3:16; 10:10)

Thoughts from the Heart

It is our coming to God, presenting our bodies a living sacrifice, holy acceptable to God which is our reasonable service...being transformed by the renewing of our minds. (Rom. 12:1-2).

Focusing on the word "Essence" (see title) meaning- the fundamental or primary nature; inherent characteristics; extract obtained by distillations, perfume, fragrance – reveals to me that, when believers come surrendering themselves to God with a grateful heart; Praising God with their whole heart (Psalm 111:1); worshipping toward His holy temple (Psalm 138:2); the Holy Spirit flows upon and within them; they draw out of the well of salvation (Isaiah 12, read entire chapter) taking on the nature and character of God. It is then the believers praise and worship goes up to God as a sweet smelling savor (a particular smell, a fragrant perfume, aroma, pleasant and enjoyable) 2 Cor. 2:15-16; Eph. 5:2; Heb. 13:15-16.

By the leading and aid of the Holy Spirit, our prayers, singing, giving, witnessing, Bible study, and our faith goes to another dimension. Even our daily occupation is geared toward praise and worship to our Heavenly Father (Eph. 6:5-6; Col. 3:17, 23-24)

Seize the moment!

The Essence of Praise and Worship Part II

Praise is an expression of heartfelt gratitude and thanksgiving for all God has done. It is physical and vocal. Psalm 34

Praise is something everyone can do, as commanded through the word of God, Psalm 150:6 "Let everything that hath breath praise the Lord." Many acknowledge the existence and the awareness of God even though they have not yielded nor committed themselves to God. This is called a Commanded Praise.

There are "Seven reasons for Praise":
1. P- It Pleases God (Psalm 69:30-31)
2. R- It Releases emotions (Psalm 103 & 106)
3. A- It gives Assurance (I John 1:9)
4. I- It Inspires the believer (Psalm 92:1,4)
5. S- It Satisfies the heart, mind and soul (Psalm 119)
6. E- It is Eternal (Rev. 4:16; 5:12)
7. S- It Saves (Romans 10:1)

The Lord desires us to praise Him, He daily showers us with His love, mercy and grace. It ought to motivate us to praise Him and give Him thanks.

Thoughts from the *Heart*

When we speak of "worship", we find there is a close relation with "Praise" until it is often difficult to determine when praise ceases and worship begins. However, the ministry of praise and the experience of worship are uniquely different although they share many common concerns, but are not the same.

Worship is expressing our admiration and commending God Himself for His person, character and attitude. We minister to God for who He is!!! Flesh cannot worship God. Only those who are followers of God i.e. sold out to God, in intimate relationship with the Holy Spirit dwelling on the inside; can truly worship Him. This is called the committed, true worshipper. It does not matter whether in the sanctuary or out of the sanctuary. Everywhere they go, in whatever they do, worship goes up to God. It is not based on musical instruments or vocal ability, and may not always be visible to those around us (Psalm 103:1).

Two words are given to help expand our understanding of worship. One is Hebrew: Shachah (shaw-khaw) meaning to bow low or to prostrate oneself, not only physically but in our hearts. Having reverential fear of God. When Abraham's servant was awed by the power of God in leading him to find Isaac's wife, he bowed low and worshipped the Lord (Gen. 24:48)

The other word is Greek: Proskuneo (pros-koo-neh) meaning to kiss the hand of, to reverence, and to adore. Giving us an invitation – O, Come, let us worship and bow down; let us kneel before the Lord our maker. For

Frances G. Core

He is our God; and we are the people of His pasture, and the sheep of His Hand (Psalm 95:6-7).

The Essence of Praise and Worship Part III
WHY PRAISE GOD

We Praise God because: (1) He commanded us to Praise Him. (Psalms 150:3); (2) He alone is Worthy to be Praised (Psalms 18:3); (3) Praise produces Strength and Power in us (Nehemiah 8:10, and Psalms 27:1), (4) Praise Stills, Stops, and Paralyzes the enemy sending him in another direction, in all situations (2 Kings 7:3-8; and 2 Chronicles 20:20-25); (5) Praise Him because He saved us (Ephesians 2:8); (6) Praise Him because He loved us (John 3:16; and Romans 5:8); (7) Praise Him for the Manner of His Love (Isaiah 53:3-5, 7-10; and John 15:13.); (8) Praise Him for the Endurance of His Love (Psalms 106:48); (9) Praise Him for the Cause of His Love (2 Corinthians 5:14-15, 18-19; and 2 Peter 3:9); (10) Praise Him for the results of Jesus' Death and Resurrection (Matthew 28:18; John 16:5, 8-11, 13-15; Acts 1:8; 2:1-4; and Hebrews 4:14-16; 5:5-10).

Our Redemption is Accepted by God through Jesus' Resurrection
(Romans 5:1-2, 5; and I Peter 1:3-5)

How We Praise God:

WORD	MEANING	SCRIPTURE
SHABACH	To Shout with a Loud Voice	Psalms 47:1; 95:2
BARACH	To Kneel in Adoration	Psalms 95:6
YADAH	Extending Hands toward God	Psalms 95:2
TODAH	Thanksgiving	Psalms 100:4
TEHILLAH	Celebrate in Songs	Psalms 95:1; 119:171
HALAH	To Celebrate	Psalms 35:18
KORAH	To Dance	Psalms 149:3

Great Is His Love

Greater love hath no man than this, that a man lay down his life for his friends. St. John 15:13

As we all know, February is noted for that special day called, "St Valentine's Day". A day for giving gifts, flowers, candy and cards with words of endearment, to those we hold dear to our hearts.

Many people will be depressed and oppressed on Valentine's day, more so than any other, because of the death of a loved one, a broken relationship with a spouse, a friend, siblings and children. Therefore, they will turn to extreme, ungodly measures as alcohol, drugs (prescription and others) to look for love in all the wrong places, to numb the pain they feel, and fill the emptiness in their hearts. I know I've been there. I found the L-O-V-E (rather, He found me), that I needed and He is real and true. His name is Jesus. I tell you of a truth, my life has not been the same.

Jesus knows the hurt and pain you feel, according to Isaiah 53: 3,4 &7; Matthew 8:17 and Hebrews 4:17. And He extends His love to everyone, "For God so loved the world, that He gave His only begotten Son, that whosoever believeth in Him, should not perish, but have everlasting life," says St. John 3:16

The Lord loves you, He really does and He loves you

unconditionally, His arms of love are open to receive you. Not only will He receive you, you can cast all your cares upon Him, I Peter 5:7. He will fill the void in your life and He will be everything you need Him to be. He will never leave you neither will He forsake you.

Jesus invites you in Matthew 11:28-29, Come unto me, all ye that labour and are heavy laden, and I will give you rest. Take my yoke upon you, and learn of me, for I am meek and lowly in heart: and you shall find rest unto your souls.

Receive His invitation and His love, it is yours; He is waiting. Only Jesus can make the difference in your life.

Whoever you are, wherever you are, this is your day, this is your hour. Seize the moment!

Prayer

Thank you, Father for your great love through Jesus. Thank you, Jesus, for giving Your life, that I might live. I receive Your love in my heart by faith and make You Lord of my life. Amen.

Keep Focused

Blessed is the man that walketh not in the counsel of the ungodly, not standeth in the seat of the scornful. But his delight is in the law of the Lord, and in His law doeth he meditate day and night. The ungodly are not so, but are like the chaff which the wind driveth away.
Therefore the ungodly shall not stand in the judgement, nor sinners in the congregation of the righteous. For the Lord knoweth the way of the righteous, but the way of the ungodly shall perish. Psalms 1:1, 2, 4-6

As I read the above "Scripture Truths"; my heart began to be saddened as I thought on the conditions of not only our nation and the world, but also...in the body of Christ. But then, I was quickened in my spirit by the Holy Ghost to "<u>keep focused</u>." (Not that I should become dull or ignorant to what is going on around me; being insensitive, uncaring, and not reaching out to others); but of "being careful of becoming self righteous and judgmental"; getting so caught-up or entangled in religion or being so politically correct to the point of taking my eyes off Jesus and the truth of the gospel. Examining myself (daily) to see if I'm in the faith, proving myself, finding out and knowing who I am in Christ Jesus and whom He will be in me.

I must hold fast the Word of God, for His Word is Truth; taking pleasure in it through faith and obedience;

allowing the will of God to be manifested in me as a faithful witness; not compromising the gospel, but speaking the truth in love; hating what God hates; loving what God loves; being a light to those who walk in darkness and telling them of God's love, grace and mercy that is given to all mankind; helping them to come to Christ in an ever yielding and loving way.

I encourage you my brothers and sisters in Christ Jesus, to stay focused; "lay hold to eternal life" (I Timothy 6:12), "looking unto Jesus, the author and finisher of our faith" (Hebrews 12:2).

Keep in mind, that the eyes of the Lord are upon the righteous and His ears are opened unto their cry. (Psalms 34:15)

Therefore, Fret not thyself because of evildoers, neither be envious against the workers of iniquity. (Psalms 37:1) The Lord knows the way of the righteous but the way of the ungodly shall perish. (Psalms 1:6)

Now unto Him that is able to keep you from falling and to present you faultless before the presence of His glory with exceeding joy. To the only wise God our Savior, be glory and majesty, dominion and power, both now and ever. Amen. (Jude 24&25)

The Danger of Legalism

In Jesus' Sermon on the Mount, (Matthew, Chapters 5-7) He reveals the truth of God's principles of righteousness, by which <u>all</u> Christians are to live through faith in Him (Galatians 2:20) and the indwelling of the Holy Ghost's power (St. John 16:13-14; Acts 1:8; Romans 8:2-14; Galatians 5:16-25)

When Jesus gave the warning in Matthew 5:20, it reads, "For I say unto you, That except your righteousness shall exceed the righteousness of the scribes and Pharisees, ye shall in no case enter into the Kingdom of heaven." This really got my attention and put a check in my spirit, of which the subject of this writing is drawn from.

One may ask, what does "legalism" have to do with my spiritual walk? What is legalism anyway? Well, I must answer you, that it has everything to do with one's spiritual walk, as well as mine, being followers of Jesus Christ.

Legalism, first of all, is not the mere existence of laws, regulations, or rules within the Christian community, But rather, it is any motive that does not stem or grow out from a living faith in Jesus Christ, the regenerating power of the Holy Ghost and the sincere desire to obey and please God. This includes our "<u>giving</u> (Matthew 6:1-4; II Corinthians 9:6-8); "<u>prayers</u> (Proverbs 15:8-29;

Frances G. Core

Matthew 6:5-11; I Timothy 2:1; Ephesians 6:18) and "fasting" (Daniel 9:3; Joel 2:12; Matthew 6:16-18).

The righteousness of the scribes and Pharisees was external only.

They appeared righteous in the eyes of people, even to those in the congregation of the church. They kept many rules, prayed, praised, fasted, read God's word, attended worship services, tithe, probably contributed to the poor (with a superior attitude). These things they did without having a change of the inward man (the heart). They substituted an outward act for the correct inner attitude.

The righteousness that God requires of every believer is a heart and spirit that is conformed to His will in faith and love, bringing about a change of attitude concerning oneself in relationship with others, that reflects on the outside (Matthew 5:16).

Jesus gave a vivid description of the scribes and Pharisees and their religious acts in Matthew 23:1-33, along with calling them a few choice names and pronouncing Woes on them eight times.

Do you want this to happen to you?

I most certainly don't want it to happen to me.

Therefore, let us "strive to enter in at the "straight" gate; Draw near with a true heart, in full assurance of

Thoughts from the Heart

faith, having our hearts sprinkled from evil conscience, and our bodies washed with pure water. ...Holding fast the profession of our faith without wavering; (for He is faithful that promised); ...Considering one another to provoke unto love and to good works. (Luke 13:24; Hebrews 10:22-24)

May God bless you.

All Praise Be Unto God

I give all glory, honor and praise to God and Jesus Christ, His Son for the Manifold blessings given to us. Yes, I can attest to the fact that we encountered much difficulties, disappointments, death of love ones and hardships. Nevertheless, I can truly say that we were and are "<u>blessed beyond measures</u>." Not because we have been so good neither deserving, but because God is good, faithful, kind and merciful. He daily loadeth us with benefits (Psalms 68:19), despite our deficiencies and misgivings.

Only as we reflect on God's benefits to us in the Scriptures, especially in Deuteronomy 8:18; Psalms 103:1-13; and Philippians 4:19, to name a few, fill our hearts with thanksgivings and praises that we cannot hold within.

Let the fruit of your lips be the praise of God daily, because "Jesus is the Reason for every Season of our lives"; His miraculous birth (Matt 1:18, 23; Luke 1:26-35, 2:1-7) and His sacrificial death (Matthew 27:32-45; Luke 23:44-46; John 19:28-30) and His glorious resurrection (Matthew 28:2-6; Mark 16:8; Luke 24:1-12; John 20:1-10) are the cause of our hope, joy, peace and salvation, now and forever, and to everyone that believe on His name.

The Lord bless thee and keep thee; the Lord make His

Thoughts from the Heart

face shine upon thee, and be gracious unto thee; The Lord lift up His countenance upon thee and give thee peace.

And... "I will bless the Lord at all times; His praise shall continually be in my mouth. My soul shall make her boast in the Lord; the humble shall hear thereof and be glad.

A New Beginning

Once again, the Lord God has blessed us to see another day. Not that we have been so good and deserving, but because…He is good: for His mercy endureth forever (Psalms 107:1); not only that – He is faithful and true (Revelation 3:7, 14; 19:11)

Having meditated on the birth of our Lord, Jesus Christ, that God the Father, so miraculously did by the Holy Spirit's conception in the virgin Mary, I began to focus on the reason or purpose of this holy birth, recorded in St Matthew 1:21 "And she shall bring forth a son, and thou shall call his name Jesus: <u>for He shall save His people from their sins</u>. John, the forerunner of Christ, saw Jesus and declared Him, "the Lamb of God, which taketh away the sins of the World." (St. John 1:29)

Man (Adam) had fallen from his holy statues, through believing satan's lies (Genesis 3:1-7), therefore, was separated from God (Genesis 3:23-24; Isaiah 59:2) Bringing sin and death upon <u>all</u> (Romans 5:12). But God's plan of salvation was already in place (Genesis 3:15; I Peter 1:18-20; Revelation 13:8)

As I meditated on Psalms 98:1, my heart rejoiced and yet rejoices, because the Holy Spirit was revealing in my spirit that it was Jesus, God's right hand, and the Holy Spirit, Himself, God's holy arm conquered the forces of darkness that overpowered us, and held us captive in sin.

Thoughts from the Heart

Everyone, who receives Jesus as Savior and Lord are never the same. For II Corinthians 5:17 declares, "Therefore, if any man be in Christ, he is a new creature; old things are passed away; behold, all things are become <u>new</u>! I repeat NEW! NEW! NEW! And continues becoming new: being "transformed by the renewing of our mind," according to Romans 12:2. This is done through reading and meditating on the Word of God daily. Forgetting those things that are behind, and reaching forth unto those things which are before, "I press toward the mark for the prize, of the high calling of God in Christ Jesus. Phil 3:4

The Final Call to the Church

In a past Sunday School quarter, there were two general topics that really stayed in my spirit – *Living Expectantly: Preparing for the Lord's Return and Visions of Hope* – messages specifically to the Church in light of the time which we now live.

People of God, the things that are happening in the world, our governing bodies of this Country, on every level, schools and homes, are very unpleasant and alarming and yet very real. At the same time God has made known to the "true" Church through His word, the things we must do and the stand we must take, against all odds, as the body of Christ; "And that knowing the time, that <u>now</u> it is high time to awake out of sleep; for <u>now</u> is our salvation nearer than when we believed. The night is far spent, the day is at hand: let us therefore cast off the works of darkness, and let us put on the armour of light. And let us walk honestly, as in the day; not in rioting and drunkenness not in chambering and wantonness, not in strife and envying. But put ye on the Lord Jesus Christ, and make no provision for the flesh, to fulfill the lusts there of." Romans 13:11-14

Many attacks from the enemy through various trials and much persecution, and temptations are coming upon the church both collectively and individually, as true believers, to make us deny our faith and lose hope.

Thoughts from the *Heart*

But God has given us mandates, in these last days and we must, "earnestly contend for the faith which was once delivered unto the saints." Jude 3. We must continue in the faith, grounded and settled, and be not moved from the hope of the gospel, which we have heard, and which was preached to every creature which is under heaven; Colossians 1:23; we are to fight the good fight of faith I Timothy 6:12, at all cost. We must, cry aloud and spare not, lifting our voices like trumpets, showing the people their transgressions, according to Isaiah 58:1.

The ultimate and final call is to be strong in the Lord, and in the power of His might. Putting on the <u>whole</u> armour of God, that we may be able to stand against the wiles of the devil … and having done all to stand, STAND!

Saints of the Most High God, we have His promises and the aide of the Holy Ghost to sustain us and guide us, as we look to Jesus the Author and Finisher of our faith.

This is a new season, this is a new day; a fresh anointing is flowing our way. All praise, glory and honor to God in the name of Jesus. And thanks be unto God which always causes us to "<u>TRIUMPH</u>"! AMEN!
Read: I Peter 1:3-7, 13-25; II Corinthians 10:3-6; Isaiah 41:10-13; 43:10; 54:17; Rev. 22: 12-14

I have enjoyed sharing with you, thoughts from the treasures of my heart and the precious Gems of the Holy Scriptures.

About the Author

Frances Green Core was born and raised in Gadsden, Alabama where she currently resides. She was educated in the Gadsden City School System, graduating from Carver High School in 1961; she completed studies in Clerical skills in 1992 at East Alabama Skills Center in Glencoe, Alabama. Ms. Core attended Easonian Baptist Bible College in 2007, and recently completed studies in Social Psychology Correspondence Courses from Stratford Career Institute in St. Albans, Vermont.

Frances has held a leadership position in the Retail, Wholesale, and Department Store Union/ AFL-CIO-CLC, Served on Prayer Call at TBN, Gadsden station; she is a former writer for The Reporter, a local newspaper. Currently, she volunteers with RSVP (Retired Senior Volunteer Program.) She is in partnership with Living Truth Christian Center, serving as Church Mother and Intercessor, under the pastorate of Apostle Amos L. Howard, Sr. Senior Pastor and Pastor Tymetric Dillon – Site Pastor.

Frances is the surviving spouse of Robert E Core after 27 years of marriage. She is the mother of six children, four sons, and two daughters, twelve grandchildren, and thirteen great grandchildren.

www.ingramcontent.com/pod-product-compliance
Lightning Source LLC
Chambersburg PA
CBHW072023060426
42449CB00034B/1883